Anselm Berrigan

Come In Alone

Seattle and New York.

Wave Books

Published by Wave Books, www.wavepoetry.com. Copyright © 2016 by Anselm Berrigan. All rights reserved. Wave Books titles are distributed to the trade by Consortium Book Sales and Distribution. Phone: 800-283-3572 / SAN 631-760X. "Copyeditor's Index" by David Caligiuri. Designed and composed by Quemadura. Printed in the United States of America. Acknowledgments: Versions of some of these poems have appeared in BOMB, frieze, Intercourse, The Recluse, West Wind Review, Cannibal, VLAK, Big Bell, Limen, Brooklyn Paramount, Washington Square Review, New American Writing, Test Centre, the Fact-Simile Poetry Trading Card Series, and Best American Experimental Writing 2015. Eternal gratitude to the Rauschenberg Residency/Robert Rauschenberg Foundation for the time, space, and facilities to make this book a thing.

Library of Congress Cataloging-in-Publication Data

Berrigan, Anselm.

[Poems. Selections]

Come in alone / Anselm Berrigan. — First edition.

pages ; cm

ISBN 978-1-940696-24-9 (limited edition hardcover)

ISBN 978-1-940696-29-4 (softcover)

I. Title.

PS3602.E7635A6 2016

811'.6—dc23

2015028436

First Edition. Wave Books 055.

9 8 7 6 5 4 3 2 1

These poems are for

June Berrigan

Sylvie Berrigan

& Karen Weiser.

in the drone, the forensic archival feast, magnanimous hemorrhoid triumphal, overly, overly pre-sent, joy a mask, eco a mask, or or or or or hepatitic imagination of used élan begets sentiment to be officious, a thing to be done dinotopic, fever balloon, sausage rye, interview to the screws, static wonder alarmed, vagrant meh, having no memories in museums used words annex light, micro pigment loans apprentice sh sh sh sh sh sh sh sh sh sh more people than today, there goes scale again, ape on fly in space, where here so little's known, to a maybe's delight, "my apple pie kicks ass", wanting all gift-giving to come down on socks, plus giving up planning to take over a world, nearby a slice for a dollar, govern warned adages, this side of it's not that you didn't pay yr fucking bill, and so less of what today is is self-evident, today being, put that name away, so many contention a glimpse … as things go … owl or etc baby or etc imitation quack to our left in the middle of a gone way being the middle of a restricted area in a nesting sign preparing body for a series of nationalized trilobitulations, delete LeBron's a trending song, he takes it space is a central factoid of bringing talents to bare projective markets, conceptually speaking I stink of pianos, in pianos, motivasions of wants hugs from J-Lo & Ice Cube, muss & dirge encore, truly it's astute to yell, at every body, at times, it's the impulse's problem, pol, secret, gray lober arrested, I divest & divest, looking for Melmoth, or a quarter, the baby takes its time, stamping duration, spit-up recognitions, no article, nor attack of fragility reading vanishing points, bouncing on this big blue ball, to quell colic at its misconception, that anaconda just

the concept must be graspable at the outset or verily most outsized as gasps freight a speech I have channels, obcific spejects, decision to be gong, to the Queen musical dimension, colored to unwilling or in fact uncornered, the issue is not credible, you daydream a nation of you, thinking intervention, thinking, intervention, thinking, intervention, thinking: intervention, matters of babied space, as to lichen

99¢ mandarin blackened red star handsome tier tumbled jasper thick squid eye moon and tilted tree sorry for working that other job I send out in notes tucked into your wish list stagger indoors imprecise holds her wrappings wolf down sweet milk april exurban sleep all day full pail & crushed on O stork mid-window Roosevelt to follow prefab gun poke the big maple smaller still is it love or it was? & that pink slip I can now swallow whole

I shit the magnanimous bed, the outer mouths, not exactly months or moths schlocking, deliberately, synth bass cruel summer style, promises the lingo to lie at least once per message, for the sake of the short leash, among other fevers needlessly treated, we see you rocking out in your with-it budget battles, it all leaks in, and on the next lap all the gongs get robbed, I was a fossilized lightning bolt siders, a video zoo herded by leaps, transfoliated, appropriate, speaking incessantly behind

any old abyss's backdoor politesse, some jobbed contingency, who became too old to be angry you guess, gradating millionish

who's beheaded by color, color & color, inskirts of stress, no of, no, stalucktus-liked, the

middling distance of reaction, defronted, republics of realty, impractically speaking, an inside of well-schooled out any old convention will do, famed Hitchcock actor dies as we squeeze a bin of life out of a few seconds, of your, I mean oh you didactic prig, pity the poor reptiles, the old meanness of magnificent feeling, the fuck all y'all part of community politics, the box of speech aiming to grope in a can-less rickshaw the puny wide-eyed ones, but and so I liked, but and so I lasciviously fantasized about, a holiday in convention article dip, bounty finagle, a shunpolite elongated mess of the familiar killing lanes, mariposa blends back a sleek scorn doily, misfried a four, seen faces facing in scamp attack of the future of materials, edges cotton, beneaths, weighted with news missed by pics, an apron lines a practice-balloon presence between her own face and a sense of, I lose purchase on that surface, rifling through hands, bottle aims its plastic contention past forming them as the ear suckles tone & fear, I get it now, I'm supposed to get it insert qualifications to extend, she searched Oh My God, we said search omigod, & the lists got weirder, the no ships of no space for broadening, insert money to begin, if you can go gnome, three-point record set in front of your parquet face, thirty-munchkin & poetically fucked off as habitat, some musics to honor by trans undisciplined lately, lack of weed one culprit, indulgence of fantasy baseball, fantasy

conflict, fantasy death, typically useful, did Morrissey just sing of getting killed by a giant deviled egg? spine hanging out

if a deeehhvuuuhhhled eeeeegggggg crashes into us? Ford Eumenides? constant election of stupid?

"like health has been an inspiration" he sd, poet shouldn't be blowing off writing to be writing, but poet has been feeling especially in the break there's little light, enough to break, what that's off remains, steering the no light I was working out on it, broken loose, not like I saw myself, the tools are cheap, as in available, usable, looking up ineffable, which sounds what it means when sung with shit, you can give yourself back, to yourself, unless, are you dead? that's an issue, binding all the times, how many yours you been in, what's a break from that flesh hotting this sounding back, negatory ops to re-up as flap or app, topaz begets peridot

dig the solid arsenic green hovered above tongue by young hand, he gave at the orifice, metal cleats for the hard concrete, substitute po-

tions fight for shipped freedoms, old news failing as blues, be the frame, I'm sorry, I hate the phone

when the snow gets cleaned my life gets ended, thrown to face, disintelligibly, that disembodied strip of match deflections, helmet scattered stacks, lines as contours, shapes heard free, from posterior dash or drizzle

she teaches herself punishment by way of self-removal from our presentable space, she plucks herself from the vicinity of

costumed now to remake her feeling, she's stubborn, she wants her own conversation, & she's right to

fight off the brokers, replace your with an article, say an inward command, undermine, in the space appearing nightly, your ability to try not knowing what'll happen, excavations should try it, activationally, try not to foresee

making 'do,' I'm sorry, for instance, to do that to you, & I'm not sorry to imagine you, no ifs about it, no fancy-faking the

po-dunk, I'd trade one street for one glen, a means, smuh, will, or an alley for a glen, or a grimy

for a bosky, for the fucked of it, know you trade word for word, this worm don't completely lack prescience, though it's fun to

ack & bony fingers tickle the first host, bill 35 a back reads, sober grid happy-bopping Brett with

blue balloon, wet gray winter garbage left out to ring in, no, relieve, the old year, propane leak, in shirley uncalled, one tours

the boroughs to preen authority, sound before scan, moving, countered in 4/4 time, what would

Rod do Peter asked wryly in reference to extraterrestrial list sex at the nothing for you sales event, let it dissipate seriously, before

shield, which will explode like loose nukes if you fire your hippy laser, you know you only shot the

flicks for the show of an unreconstructed it, whispering shadows, dear friends, a no-fly zone calls us, outcomes will not politely elude us

if I sot, shall I succor, "on my mind", or, er, yours, er's an ill use of space, you could drop

turkey bacon there, or orf, or Boethius, proto fave dude in the pen, pesteration over cluster tones on the halfnowness, images of memories, vice versa or otherwise, domestic thuggery's kluge, in uniform battles itself, for victory, actual user, compensated for appearing, acting, being directed, resembling nature, surrounding temporary objects washed instead of hugged, the scrubbled silence, candle, glass, spicy red shit in plastic eternity container, we sit here looking like I'm doing, approachably, this, you or I to love, the sounds we don't intend, decades from a starry bunting, this rash owns finality less weapons, whistle blown through supposing a list-ening to breathing, crack break down transition, less extension, supposing, less transpaque, one does not control an army of imaginations, or ones do, suppose dignity, less conversation, control panels in on itself, they say this deal makes me felt, suppose subject's another says a cover, a tuck rule, a meditating zamboni

I hear the old edge of bad production values waiting for baby to leave cramp expansion & give me back my decadent abjection popularly deemed responsibility, death to or by syllables, with eyes of fury spilling post-emo cheques from speakers, a column worked it out that feeling & reasoning like to lick one another in the echoey eco-corn syrupy spots, & that was cool, but then I knew of nature's horrors & weirdo powers &

of it must be said axe of too I've been treating the known badly drifting from its

less tangible perimeter no I don't think alcoholic isolation is too bereft a condition to be so unsympathetic as to

kill off hope for the work Jack or Jack but you did do it wrong and I may do it

wrong too though I doubt it much to some of the time I'm still letting myself into this form this variating wobbling for sale under hard core formica on time for the toddled eval sweat-science

overly beaten by its reads, hey A-Rod, what's the deaglio with ebb gulfing the pock? mitigated by his or hers bark and saw

accentuation? please consider offing our troubled backbiting phrase or clause of attack

the populist deliberates angle by which to slice, an expendable alley of lives, here we go again, meaning, there I go again diminutive singularity trafficking in slight excursions to tropical corners damn few & they're all dead

awake to be dear at not cost to be unclear at no cost to be deerlight at no costs to be queer at no cost to be freer at no to be Pam

Grier at no cost to be general vermeers at all or no costs to be gear bent on active disinterest in the

arming thing while expectations of thing diminish to obituary studies in miniature kitchens to make space within to for to's sake and its goldenplacemat, oh window, make me a meanie, a production membrane of messianic society, flossy mythos of a clock-sick stucco exit frame, with empowered props & their realist two-tone cills just begging for intimacy, like a good little flame, sold to preserve saving, recs & blurbs & gimpy tantrums, the giving of birth in the boxy tub, a present marginalized by demons of exterior register, the cowled worm's mine, the singer from the Buzzcocks sounds pretty joyful singing about his sleepless nights & I get pretty happy thinking about revisiting the melancholy in Saturn's rings, neither fact of which nor factoid of what melt factory of whence ekes any of us alike, wry ruins porn pisses off inhabs of ruined places, that ain't like anything, upper limit decay/lower limit free for all, unlike this current I of poctalypse had been happening & this is the aftermath? zebra stalls my favorite plastic pict blooming, feelings causing flab attack future no budgie, here's your purty red handmade hat with red pom poms ya big sass bag renderer follower numberer of things, attack & decay, proof that butt, olds, fashioned linkage, and when the light gets turned on, to be conscious waste, you better carry, you mean, the era my efficiency level's stooped, accounting for a cordial condescending knot, our home's a non-repeating son's divemare, hangover begets turnover, yet yer site gets no spasm to co-own in the rolling plunk of the neo-schooled, weird shit going glass to chop the venerable strum in its steep steppe a gbs knot resistant to the legal no I'm not quite getting inside the phantom cough, the plastered box no wheel but deep, no new, she detects more than me, but she may detect more than I believe I give off, a relationship to no, internal, speaking, I know well not to hope to feel so known, projecting, as with living, but I want you to know, not so much to be, being that, no matter what surface climbs up to ride along, it's a good mess, I get it that way, out on the skirts, the we who lives with me, from the off-center deranged mirror factory, used books anonymous, teaching three-year-olds to waste water's a start bleeding crank, fighting strangers, "my mind is my friend" this guy I recognize from an eighties version e.v. says I'm just like him tho the harmonized regulation fast still gets in the way "from time to time", who made that into commonality, cut & run greets cut & gloat, strategy sausage ploweth into the lately pangs of outrageous ambition, one chooses to affect taking part in space or handles limited choices, no, both, ehs?, all in all in, you don't, get to, don't you, look at me, a half thought, don't be a did it wrong, so goes ubiquity, biquity, quity, the premise of an open box as trad display of public possible affection caged religion, the pleasure of a luxurious sense of oppression, the first glo habit turning exquisite grime into corners, the annotated worm community leaving signs in shot space, naming colors can't quite qualify as translation, in shelled space, now I'm one & now I'm done no trade clauses, no certification of brain waves, dunks meet discovery, to take effect would you, tight-ass billionaire baby, acquire mellow for half yer face? pre-labor stress with all-star fatigue as day nice decay & do relate? o hook, red pointy pussy willow blanched, stripped, weirding pop diselaborates a video scored pasting, fresh from the barbed dumbs shop, the sputnik snow job seen from the houseless grab, dig the vehic-les hiding, nothing in that voice, hearing images, don't do food talk when she wakes up a crank on the floor, give that pressure back to this boxy atmosphere, transparents making it up to go, outnumbered by things depiction's duration toasts a skyway's formal slide out in that terrestrial scuzz sense of a cheap open queue for grease one shops with slop with government warning in wobbly letters disavowing their hypnocritical no source, old man June vibrating asleep in her starry-eyed gleam: my fingers I mean dese tings do dis? all the vanishing poops of fact colorate the living floor upon which she was muscularly made born the eyelid clamor drinking a dork's snipe scotch, a weathered Tiepolo's cleaved skywriting self-defenestrating budgpocalypstick stacks, walker says we're broke but he ain't, the donor organs agree, cost-spatially fresh set of eyes, percolating in K's belly, you mean I gotta get my shit together again? to sleeplessly be getting shit together, shit & shit & piss & shit together & gether get & to & her & her & her too, & me on prime a walk away with vanilla place re-reckoning a reckoned space to make caves

for a metta world peace blomb plug allegiance to tinks I blew off realities and all other tinks redubbed mesself someone

else which was not unlike will being thirty-eight janitoring bumpkins such as

myself to needlepoint dreams of quality control for pain at the pump — is that what the graphic says? pain at the pump all your exuberant dismay, no, sir, I don't wish, & by the way the weather's none of your fucking bizness, the what ever happened to scan makes a changey entrance, & I'd like but won't engage further the money part of the new strafe, wreck of a shambles the clause knows, getting to have gotten around the pinch she's all will, inertia, need & the various formal clichés around growth, you know you wanna say the w the sword in of a person, with or without character, than it used to be, now it's more fun to brigadoon than it used to be, & it's more fun to forestall doom than it used to be, it's more fun to care specifically than it used to be, & I have to say it, it's more fun to keep secrets than it used to be, & it's more fun to be lazy & stupid than it used to be, it's more fun to talk to yourself openly than it used to be, & it's more fun to be a shambles

endlessly from Western Division Standings, would you like another zap right between the bodywork? there's no, there's no, there's no, frameshield, I replied, with lego aphasia sprinkled on our mourning disas- ter, ergo, to live without a set of masks for unprecedented occasion would be too little for me, as I fumble to enable my own shade of neutral, in the sink of roman terror, getting thee to a livery, ordering out able claim of face brokering severity, postal-races implicit in furtherly dreamed seizures of homage to how it was when how was how's servant in tow, striding indecently between bombs, generous when needed with dissolution, cross a line/any line, it's the replacement dream, American affect in long form, & now to offer explanation in exchange for permission to reenter duration's mirror as personage reframed, hung for ace of pentacles I bottled my so-called strangeness to pour into a wordless wreck affecting known space to get an orange fruit bowl filled version of your approaching the earliest empty donnybrook we hear the fallen but for the fuckers address to whom be blacked out as no as now back around & pls disavow the silt of this here ribald command to overhear for the voices resides: subotica subspace being a flung pal video, she's a pretty little booger, flying should feel like it, cocktail party sheep packing heat, I do doth diddly recognize yr genus, next to apples in stereometric space a pansy kiss glazed with tranquility, fear itself a limited run comic collaged from a version of sustainable self for money see electable affinities our trivia categories tonite: general knowledge, ironic hats, the inflammable, a public's left to unknown, irreducible pets, & pricks on went apeshit on ares and asgard in c, deerhead in daytime woke up and knew it had to be foreground & background at once, first aid for choking, the clause clamp clueless in space exploration, one investigates & says I investigate, death to analogy not with, a study in embarrassment, the porous choices dressed to media rez, look like no mail for days expecting checks the newer baby goes batshit in heat if held the sentry surfaces of circular pale-lit pale ale lamps, fruitful in daylight flat to brick, the wall perpendicular

to ave, behind a variant quote, exaggerated morbidity as underrated as a human rain delay, cleaved from listlike memory

with the lustlike veneer of a happy smudge the pies vie for ғɪʀsт! rollover, the thunder sighs

spit bubbles on elephant fuzz, a tucked assuage sausages a drop off, the zebra hide influences upholstery as per bat wings ground beastie round a heather, beat ye outta ye, time depiction crashing, trained route a given off green slump, permanent derail breeding affect & where it goes I follow, I follow, I follow an unlit fetid massageway, having thoughts like any brother of wood, craven breaded anypart, this hear nurture patio pressurized by the looming threatness of subdivided as steady dryhumper of dimes I see your roo-shaped cumulus clouds turning wilde

did just enough to enter their hosts, they sculpted my head from life, they doused it with nontoxic repellency they made shacks filled with pillows of come, they tangled with destitute animation slaves, they drank port at the feet of Ben Frank-lin, they totally bewore lack of grace, they performed their selves by being them, they went unnoticed, they admitted to piecing it together for the sake of trauma, their profiles escaped tangibility, they turned down sound at movies, they the nonstop border, a case of speece hashed out as confrontational sieve, liked it/didn't get it, now we're back to looking for a working space out, staff making sameness pay, but their somethings are not, fos-flops the model making, hiding a lamebrain, missed both memorials, standings ready to bring all the money ones can steal to an index holding hostage a host of anti-monitors banging against

.

between us twenty hundred translated opening mid-woodses ago, pre-trading Ubaldo to Lake Erie from Colorado, I am a maiden exemplar counter to your conference & its teeming placards of neckless neon in the vizio, a copy of a feel response to momentary status flashes back at me, three-year-old's of course letting out seams galore tweaking hamstrings in practice Jorge Harry coos in Norman's about the space

I emulated Raphael by toying with him, give off: finality, no sell, a simple scream on the corner at any old passerby, its carry-on, free of charge, like the hen said, self-cancellation got no truck unless some real oil gets thematized this pictorial pathos makes me feel felt up in front of a photo of found: America's most hated upgrade, the object neglecting self-destruction for the moment while in it would you like to be a fairy or zebra little thru daddy?

in a dunce hat, your tick looks like a pumpkin pre-positioned to mutually exploit invention, you think you got your own unmade space-time-based maroon objection, that anxiety's an armchair hugging back, take the cartoon, the practical secret — o guise of mind — out of the song & pet urgency oinks in the techno-slumster afternoon, here a horn I would I were a weedling, your shit sits there so it or its bleeder supported news goes, the cuppeth wants more money, the mark wants more moneyed appreciation my collection of toots & totes tells me at odd hours, feeling pre-material unlike chicken nuggets in spherical pictorial spirit, but fry &, having breaded, that thing's right wing, the character I will certainly — depot man? — happily eat that wing, besauced in convention on as a field of targets, happily inscribed, earning variations on nothing, sounds of an open disembod

ied mic downstairs, closed corset of design getting all the data roles pliably funded to disbelieve at a monument's notice I

diggeth being subjected to a doe's planar tumble trouble, official sustainable wobble provider for the

Twins, Tintoretto falling bodjects, threes on sleeves across a pictorial diamond beamed to Orchard, among other places one sits in the idea of an embedded quack in the abstracted black pigment, old pagan midday cuts an imaginary throat to hide a wretched desire — *wretched* — there's a word I hadn't ever heard aloud until the other day, lacking enigmas like a bummer, a clear illusion in the wiry mouth a ding, Porky Duck deserves a secret harbor to here be the way Stella knew Donald dig dug give off, file a fund raising campaign for honey basted cryptics who need your self-perceived perversions to unwind, to strive like black crocs, like painting with black arch, like still life with chair caning like mellow crypt, like compatibility modes to be real, outside but in extension of given space up your urbane choice, choose your own mangled indentity to be fonted in the crap ding, see notation's poodle, ignore its a manatee beisbol league's adamantium simplicity of life's lifelike costume tuned to quotation ultimately rebooted the various trust covers call it my paint feintfully being I unless asked & even then it's not exactly that, don't reflect pain on the face-side of blank with cap italicized b traded this morning Antonio Bastardo & John Mayberry Jr. for Sergio Santos in Frozen Ropes was in a model thruway from sump to sling no purification by intrusion that's the ticket ex

amines edges with fingers all the gathering bickering imbibing & lo-falutinin was just prelude to diving into

some stranger's sturdy hedge that where's the cyclical obstinacy of haggard prep all rats

abandon stump, we were doing skeletal shading under the compressed ghost of a song thing space wasn't there but fucking treat the digital animals buadly gaining a just watched sparkle the oversized helmet

bouquet to nirvana discursive means what again arrived in quotation according to every working memory available to dream

spicy belly super duper super duper super violence animated zips windshield comacosmotic (un)licensed

extra ball at forty-seven million seven hundred thousand represents the recent extinguished past emphasized start to choking on in nondreams agh! stems from the fact that one never pans in real life anyways sylvie's implicit use of kandinsky's shapes turning towards falconry on the make above this leaking bus looking at all these dragons & one is miniature with the breathed fire this hard rubber orangey protrusion & that's not the pride dragon the ewing dragon that's the scary one you're day was misdirected anger, now & later colored taffy tough paint, ings, the pictorn planes diving out of plaster depths, with a delicate emotional poise unafraid of avoiding pronouncements' poky potbelly & backup aves something between chinchilla & rabbit chilling on a rockified ledge solicited by ram & carrier pigeon, I don't know that I dream or think in comprehension love, we can give each other filled-in stars, zero to five, all go again, besides which, uneasy, even, at the back of the mind, especially, got to pee

fill you in when I'm back, fantasy, in the scheme of things, we do and we do, hard time stay put, speaking of near past, the

stitches drop, free later, like drift, starting to, me Exactly, anyhow, put hand out to break the

fall, butts, too, get a bite later, ready in a few, back shortly, well you may ask, that Sunday, find a quarter

practical, on the inside, but am so, on the outs, & vice versa, which I also hate

the other page is wet, caravaggio wants to be here, true, but the rate's for a week, now this one's wet, peche in candied daylight

you could have fucking forwarded it to me, hand in revision, fantast, spaceless

mouth, bummer's a lean, a method of croak, discrete bramble, hello kitty hairpin, jabbing thigh removable, I hate it that I'm not scrotum radiance alert, death's dog food, necromancy's survey brains, all feeling like overpriced tenements aghast at the cost of a glimpse, you were being wry in your bonus, according to an otherwise ordinary occupation, I'm smiling at my reflection, as you pull my hair to scold me for something I already forgot I did, it's so nice to be happy this way, in & of at once continuously preparing the verge, being a cigarette of quality, on

enough to adapt I'm hungry enough to listen to nod to put work into changelings

push the figuration button under the blushes and over par as a guillotinist I seek the vessel of the body for purposes

of drop off service & distant voicing requisite ouch and so forth broken into man you'll

be a there I could never be a girlhood soon & I'm insulted by your excess of believability I can afford to be elected I'm isolated up a flight in this donnybrook vikings in the antelight turn to ponder buzzer yes bill well no I never but have dived under a buzzer yes very swell pulling walls toward your remembered hell which is neither prescient nut nor bean spasms on e-bay pushing this blue octopus in a blue stroller through concrete colored slush to pour vinegar chutney on a major stylistic transposition, it's not you, it's your throughline, your voiceless holes tripping of the space ghost because there was no reason to put it a bit on the side, I got to the anatomy & I feel myself almost getting flustered I really could never get hold of it since I have no preference or so called sense of it did one thing for me: eliminate composition, arrangements, relationships time, all this silly talk about line, voice and form because that was the thing I wanted to get hold of I put it in the center

ab bodjects

- babied — 10
- ack — 22
- boros — 22 (.not ":boroughs"?)
- a.x.f — 27
- budgocalypsstick — 40
- blomb — 41
- anypart — 50
- sewore — 51
- anti-monitors — 52
- béisbol league — 60
- buadly — 62

jkl [ave(s)

- -like — 49
- lo-faluting — 61

cd comacosmatic — 62

- dinotopic — 6
- canless — 14
- cheques — 26 / checks — 48
- deaglio — 28
- cills — 30
- divemare — 33
- C-row — 33
- day glo — 37
- colorate — 39
- changey — 42
- come — 51

mn negatory — 19

- meh — 6
- micro — 6
- motivasions — 8
- mid-window — 11
- neo-schooled — 33
- no source — 39
- metta — 41 (world peace)
- mesself — 41
- massageway — 50
- mid-weedses — 53
- mic

efg

- eco — 6
- gift-giving — 7
- gray —
- gradating — 13
- eval — 28
- goldenplacemat — 30
- gbs — 33
- e.v. — 35 ("eighties version"?)
- ehs? — 36
- fos-flops — 52 (fosbury flop)

op poctalypse — 32

- outsized — 10
- oversized — 62
- O — 11, 38, 55
- oh — 14, 116, 30
- omigod — 16
- ops — 19
- po-dunk → podunk (?) — 21
- proto fave dude — 23
- orf — 23
- post-emo — 26

hi

- hepatitic — 6 (?)
- ifs — 21
- half- — 23
- hippy → hippie (?) — 23
- inhabs — 31
- half thought — 36
- hypocritical — 39
- hungable — 45
- ings — 64

qr

- re-reckoning — 41
- rollover — 49
- roo-shaped — 50
- rockified — 64
- pics — 15
- pictorn — 64
- pict — 32
- peche — 66
- pre-trading — 53 / pre-positioned — 55
- pls — 46
- plowerth — 35
- pre-labor — 37

s t subotica — 46
speece — 52
sh
trilobitulations — 8
transfoliated — 13
shunpolite — 15
sd (said) — 17
smush — 21
shirley — 22
transpague — 25
trad — 36
scuzz — 39

numbers / sections
.99 — 11
4/4 time — 22
→ "4" ?
→ 4

u v w x y z ye ~50[2]
yr (your) — 7, 47
y'all
word for word — 21
variating — 27
vermeers — 29
vizio — 53
yer — 33, 37
throughline — 69
towards — 63, 69
tonite — 47 / tho — 35
thru — 54

names — places, things
hello kitty hairpin — 66

Orchard ~57 →

punctuation / ligatures
. ellipsis — 8[2]
etc., — 8[2],
space-time-based — 55
agh! — 63
Jr. (no commas) — 60

66, 67, 68[2], 70
55, 56[2], 60, 63[2], 64[3],
43[5], 45, 47, 48[2], 50, 53,
35[2], 37, 38, 40[8] 42[2],
21, 22, 26[5], 30[3], 31, 32[2]
• ampersand — 9, 11[2], 16[3]

caps / small caps
sputnik — 38
scotch — 40
to brigadoon (verb) — 43
lego aphasia — 44
ares and asgard — 48
me Exactly — 65
vikings — 69
april — 11
cap italicized b — 60

names — persons
J-Lo ~9
A-Rod — 28
K's belly — 40
Sylvie — 63
guillotinist — 68
Tiepolo's — 40

ornaments / other
dese tings do dis — 39
tinks — 41[2] / tings — 39
working space out — 52
- eth
— ploweth (35),
— doth (47),
— cuppeth (56),
— I diggeth (57)